THE**JAZZ**FUNK BASS**METHOD**

Master the Art of Grooving, Funky Basslines with Jamiroquai's Paul Turner

PAUL**TURNER**

FUNDAMENTAL**CHANGES**

The Jazz Funk Bass Method

Master the Art of Grooving, Funky Basslines with Jamiroquai's Paul Turner

ISBN: 978-1-78933-441-8

Published by **www.fundamental-changes.com**

Edited by Tim Pettingale

www.fundamental-changes.com

Join our free Facebook Community of Cool Musicians

www.facebook.com/groups/fundamentalguitar

Instagram: **FundamentalChanges**

For over 350 Free Guitar Lessons with Videos Check Out

www.fundamental-changes.com

Bass transcription & notation by Johnny Cox

https://johnnycoxmusic.com

Contents

Introduction

Welcome to The Jazz-Funk Bass Method. This book is all about developing the skills to create grooving basslines that will complement a tune and sometimes (like many of the great basslines in music history) be the main hook or feature.

I generally don't like to categorise music too much, and I always try to be open minded with my listening, but we had to give this book a title! If I think about music that has a syncopated, catchy rhythm, which also has some jazz-influenced harmony, or is used as a vehicle for improvisation, then I think it's fair to call it Jazz-Funk! I like lots of different music, but I particularly like jazz, and I love funk. All musical genres can seem a little restrictive in their definition, yet they are vague at the same time, because boundaries are often blurred. Let's go with jazz-funk and I think we'll all know the vibe.

In this book I'll show you some of my favourite approaches for warming up and playing in the pocket with great feel. You'll also learn a structured approach for creating basslines from scratch by combining essential components that I'll break down for you.

By the end of this book, you'll have learned what can make a bassline truly funky and memorable, and will have added some cool, creative ideas to your bass vocabulary. You'll also understand how introducing articulation into your basslines can add character and transform a plain idea into a hook or exciting highlight.

I hope that the main takeaway for you, however, is that you'll develop the ability to internalise these rhythms, feels, and grooves so that they *feel* natural to you, and you can use them spontaneously when improvising.

Enjoy your playing!

Paul Turner

Get the Audio

The audio files for this book are available to download for free from **www.fundamental-changes.com**. The link is in the top right-hand corner. Click "Download Audio" and choose your instrument. Select the title of this book from the menu, and complete the form to get your audio.

We recommend that you download the files directly to your computer (not to your tablet or phone) and extract them there before adding them to your media library. If you encounter any difficulty, we provide technical support within 24 hours via the contact form.

For over 350 free guitar lessons with videos check out:

www.fundamental-changes.com

Join our free Facebook Community of Cool Musicians

www.facebook.com/groups/fundamentalguitar

Tag us for a share on Instagram: **FundamentalChanges**

Chapter One – Groove Essentials

When I'm teaching students in a workshop setting, I often begin by asking the question, *What makes a bassline groovy?*

This usually elicits a range of responses, and people will describe "groove" in many different ways, but I think it can be agreed that the ultimate quality the musical part must possess is that it *feels good.* Any bassline we create should help the listener to "feel" the rhythm of the music and should make them want to move with it. Groovy doesn't always mean funky, but funk needs to groove!

To discover how we can make our basslines groove, we're going to explore what I like to call the *bass rudiments.* Just as drummers study drum rudiments on the snare, working through all the options for placing subdivisions to the beat, we can do the same on bass.

To make a bassline groove, it's essential for us to get to grips with note *placement*, but just as importantly, note *length*. Then we can explore the many ways in which we can vary and personalise any group of notes and generate endless bassline ideas.

To start us off, let's just play a series of steady 1/8th notes. Each note is played *staccato* i.e., cut off as soon as it's played, rather than being allowed to ring.

Example 1a

The first thing we can do to add some groove to a constant stream of 1/8th notes is to alter the length of certain notes.

In Example 1b, every 1/8th note that falls on the downbeat is played staccato, while each note that falls on the off-beat is allowed to ring for its full duration.

We count a bar of 1/8th notes as, "1 & 2 & 3 & 4 &".

The staccato notes are played on the 1, 2, 3, 4, and the held notes are played on every "&".

Example 1b

That was a simple example of how we can begin to change the "feel" of a rhythm, even just using 1/8th notes. We could play around with 1/8th note placement for quite a while, but many more options open up when we think of bassline construction in 1/16th notes, and begin to combine the two.

We count a bar of 1/16th notes as, "1-e-&-a, 2-e-&-a, 3-e-&-a, 4-e-&-a".

Learning to access the four possible note placements on each beat is one of the keys to mastering syncopation, a.k.a. *groove*.

Here's a simple but effective 1/16th note bassline. Here we play the *first* two 1/16th notes in beat 1: "1-e".

Then, we play the *last* two 1/16th notes in beat 2: "&-a".

Then, we play nothing and leave space on beats 3 and 4.

Here's how we count that groove. The notes we're playing are highlighted in bold type:

1-**e**-&-a, 2-e-**&-a,** 3-e-&-a, 4-e-&-a.

This is more complicated to explain in words than it is to hear! As soon as you listen to the audio, you'll nail it, but at this stage it's important for you to understand how we are creating a groove from note placement.

Example 1c

Let's create a variation of the previous example by adding notes to make a more complex syncopated pattern. We're going to keep the previous rhythm intact, but add notes in the space we left on beats 3 and 4. We'll still count the overall rhythm as…

"1-e-&-a, 2-e-&-a, 3-e-&-a, 4-e-&-a"

…but we'll be playing 1/8th notes during beats 3 and 4 to create a more interesting rhythm.

In Example 1d we're placing accent notes on the "&" of beat 3, and the "e" of beat 4 (highlighted in bold):

1-**e**-&-a, 2-e-**&-a,** 3-e-**&**-a, 4-**e**-&-a.

The first 1/8th note we've added is played staccato on the "&" of beat 3.

The second is a dotted 1/8th note (the value of an 1/8th note plus half the note value again).

Once again, it's easier to hear how this should sound rather than read it, so before you attempt the exercise, have a good listen to the audio and begin to internalise the rhythm.

Playing a staccato 1/8th note, followed by a longer dotted 1/8th note just after the downbeat, causes it to "float" over the rest of the bar, creating a strong sense of groove.

Example 1d

Let's develop this idea further.

Here is a variation on the previous groove. Strong 1/8th notes (first played staccato then allowed to sound for their full value) anchor down the groove, while 1/16th note accents – all played on off-beats – add to the syncopation.

We're adding a new technique this time, which is a great tool to use when playing funk basslines. In bar two, *ghost notes* are introduced just before each pair of 1/16th notes, to add even more syncopation to the groove.

To play a ghost note, keep playing the rhythm with the plucking hand but mute the note with the fretting hand fingers by lifting them lightly from the fretboard. Just a subtle movement is required. Avoid unwanted harmonics by not lifting the fretting finger too high. It can help to mute the string with an adjacent finger. Ghost notes are very useful for adding dynamics into your basslines, but they can be overused, so be tasteful.

Example 1e

After the previous, highly syncopated examples, here's one that highlights how to make a bassline groove by controlling note lengths.

The idea here is to play mainly 1/8th notes (apart from the quick 1/16th note phrase that ends each bar), but to play some of them staccato, while allowing others to ring for their full value. This creates a sense of momentum for the line.

Played over a Gm7 vamp, we're mostly using a simple root note plus 5th pattern, but we're also adding notes from the G Natural Minor scale (F, Bb, A) to create a riff.

Example 1f

Here's a much more syncopated approach, also using notes from the G Natural Minor scale.

To create a nice little tension, we're also including a chromatic approach note in this idea. A chromatic or "passing" note is one that doesn't belong to the parent key we're playing in. In the key of G Minor, we'd expect to find an Eb note, but here we play a chromatic E note leading to an F scale tone in the middle of the bar.

In jazz or fusion this is called *targeting*. The idea is that we target an "inside" sounding scale tone by playing an "outside" sounding chromatic note, located either a half-step below or above the target. This creates a brief moment of tension that is quickly resolved.

This line creates momentum and energy by playing the root note on beat 1, but placing the subsequent note (Bb, the b3) before beat 2, on the "a" of beat 1 (i.e., "1-e-&-**a**").

Example 1g

Example 1h is a great bassline idea to loop around for practice, to help get you warmed up and playing in the pocket.

This highly syncopated idea starts in bar one with two 1/8th notes, beginning on beat 1 and placing the second note on the "1-e-**&**-a".

All the other notes are arranged around the off-beats, so that only the first note of the bar falls on the beat. This is a two-bar loop and, in the second bar, the first note is omitted, so that no notes are played on the beat.

For most bass players, it's a moment of revelation when we realise that the space we leave is as important as the notes we play, and often more so! Placing notes on off-beats allows kick drum and snare hits to punch through the mix as the bassline weaves around them. This brings separation and clarity to the groove, and it's the interaction of the drums and bass that really brings the funk.

Example 1h

Based on the previous idea, this bassline adds additional chromatic approach notes that target the chord tones of the underlying Gm7 harmony (G, Bb, D, F).

In beat 2 of bar one, a chromatic F# connects the b7 (F) and root (G). In beat 3, a chromatic C# connects a C scale tone with the 5th (D) of Gm7. At the end of bar one spanning into bar two, a descending chromatic phrase uses a non-scale tone B to connect C and Bb (b3).

Example 1i

Over the course of the last few examples we established a solid bassline idea and arrived at Example 1i. We got there by starting with some very basic rudiments, then developed the idea through several iterations.

This is a good process for crafting a bassline:

- Start simple

- Begin to build on and embellish your idea

- Then, continue to self-edit until you've got a solid idea that works

- Recognise the way subtle changes can make a line feel different, such as anticipating the downbeat (beat 1) with a pushed 1/8th or 1/16th note

One thing I often get students to do when they've created a bassline like this, is to play it through different key centres, moving it around the neck. This is enlightening because it's good to hear how the bassline sounds in other areas of the fretboard, in different octaves, and with different timbres. It's also a great way of really understanding how the intervals contained in the line work together.

One way to approach this is to come up with a chord progression, then apply the bassline to it, making any adjustments needed to accommodate each new chord.

A good tip here is to keep your progression to chords of the same quality to begin with (all minor chords, for example). That way, the fundamental idea of the bassline can stay the same and we only have to worry about connecting it to each new chord.

Here's the idea from Example 1i played over a chord progression.

After the G minor riff, I decided to move down a whole step to F minor. After that I moved down a 5th to Bb minor, then up a 4th to Eb minor, then looped around back to the beginning.

The real challenge with this kind of idea comes from seamlessly moving from one chord to the next. Play through the whole exercise slowly a few times and get the shape of it under your fingers before increasing the tempo.

Example 1j

Let's take a deeper look at this bassline and I'll explain my strategy of adapting it to connect each chord in the progression.

This is a two-bar bassline. The idea is that we begin in bar one by playing the root of the chord in octaves.

Then, in bar two, we play the b3 of the chord in octaves for variation. It's easy to spot the chord tone targeting approach of the riff, where we either walk up or down chromatically. What makes this line funky is that while we hit those roots and b3s on the downbeat, the chromatically targeted chord tones are all played on the off-beat.

The bassline follows an identical pattern for each chord change, apart from the last three notes. These three notes (at the end of bars two, four, six and eight) are used to target the root note of the next chord. So, it's only these notes that need to be tweaked in order to target the root of the next chord.

An idea like this tests our fretboard knowledge and visualisation of the neck. We need to think ahead and be able to identify the root notes of chords on the higher strings on the fly. Try this process with any bassline you've come up with and use it as a practice routine.

You will have noticed that while many of these examples feature cleanly plucked notes, we have started to introduce a little articulation via some hammer-ons. We will explore articulation techniques more fully later, but to close out this chapter here's another idea that can really add to the feel of the groove: the *legato slide*.

In this example I slapped and plucked, and used slides to add a different flavour to the part. The legato slides add a lilt and almost make the note feel like it's "wider" by slurring into the target note. This all adds personality to the bassline and can transform how it sits alongside other instruments in the band mix.

For the slides, slap the first note indicated in the TAB, then slur into the target note. All the slaps and plucks are highlighted in the notation.

Example 1k

Chapter Two – Bassline Generation from Simple Motifs

We've looked at the importance of note placement and note length to create strong, grooving basslines, but how can we create our own bassline ideas from scratch? In this chapter, we'll look at how to take a simple idea then progressively embellish it as a way of creating unlimited musical ideas.

The concept of using "cells" or "motifs" – both terms that describe a phrase made from just a few notes – is one that runs throughout jazz-fusion, and is a great way of grounding our musical ideas. A practical example of this is to focus on just a few notes in a particular zone of the neck, then base our musical ideas around it. We can add as much embellishment as we like, adding in extra notes and articulation, but structuring our ideas around the original motif anchors the bassline and glues everything together.

In the examples that follow, our focus will be the 3rd fret zone, and the notes G, Bb and F – the root, b3 and b7 of a Gm7 chord. From this cell we'll build lots of different variations.

First, here is the starter idea that sets out the basic feel of the groove. It begins with a dotted 1/8th note, followed by a 1/16th note, then a staccato 1/8th note. A short embellishment at the end of bar two helps the idea to loop around and makes it feel like a two-bar idea, rather than a repeat of bar one.

However, by leaving out the embellishment in bar four, the loop can be lengthened to four bars. This is a basic example, but this approach allows us to keep some catchy repetition while stretching out the line.

You'll notice that later examples in this chapter use chromatic notes – a common device in jazz phrases, melodies, and walking basslines. Adding some passing notes to our syncopated lines can give some jazz to the funk (see what I did there, haha!)

Example 2a

Here's the first variation on this motif. The first thing to notice here is that we've relocated the Bb note onto the low E string and targeted it with a legato slide. Then we've relocated the F note onto the A string. Using this alternative fingering eliminates the need for string crossing and makes any embellishments easier to play.

In this example we're also fleshing out the motif by repeating it within a bar and adding select notes, which come from the G Dorian scale (G, A, Bb, C, D, E, F).

Example 2b

This example changes the rhythm of the original motif by adding space after the note on beat 1. Although this bassline sounds quite different to where we started, we can still hear the original motif and visualise the shape of it on the fretboard.

This time, the first note of the four-bar loop is played as a staccato 1/8th note. In every subsequent bar this is replaced by a held 1/4 note. And, rather than having the repeating motif, it is just played once and a new ending to the phrase has been added.

Example 2c

Once we come up with an idea we like, we can continue with it and then vary the new idea. Example 2d is a development of Example 2c. We're hitting 1/4 notes on beat 1 every time now and modifying the end of the phrase with a short descending chromatic run (adding a passing B note between two scale tones).

Example 2d

This next line keeps the idea from bar one of the previous example, but adds a new phrase in bar two. The rhythmic phrasing of this new idea is kept in bar four, but different notes are played. This shows that motifs can be *note-led* or *rhythm-led* and this allows us to explore alternative ways to keep our basslines catchy but harmonically varied.

Example 2e

This idea takes the line from bar one of the previous example and repeats it until we end with a slight variation at the end of bar four, which turns the idea into a more seamless loop.

Example 2f

For a more radical take on the motif, we can do two simple but effective things.

First, we can change one of the notes of the motif. Instead of our G, Bb, F cell, here we're using G, Bb, D (root, b3 and 5th of Gm7).

The second, more dramatic change, is to relocate the motif to a different place in the bar.

Moving a motif phrase to a different place in the bar is called *displacement* and it's a technique we can get unlimited mileage out of. Moving a phrase by just one beat, or more radically to cross a bar line for example, is a great way to generate new ideas.

Here we're moving the strong G root note to beat 2 of the bar, preceding it with a short chromatic phrase that targets the root note an octave above. This gives the groove a completely different feel.

Example 2g

After we've been playing lots of different variations of our bassline, we can always return to the core motif to ground the harmony. Here we're back to where we started, but with some added embellishments in the higher register, so that we're using more of the range of the neck.

Example 2h

Hopefully you can see that by using these simple techniques, you're able to generate almost endless musical variations of your basslines.

For practice, put on a medium tempo drum groove and invent your own simple riff or motif.

Now spend some time creating variations based on that idea using the different techniques we've discussed:

- Explore an alternative fingering to open up other embellishment ideas

- Use repetition and add in other notes to enhance the motif

- Change the feel by mixing up staccato and longer held notes

- Add in some chromatic passing notes to enrich the harmony

- Keep the rhythm of your motif but use different notes

- Experiment with displacement by playing the motif in different parts of the bar

- Lock in your ideas and repeat then expand. Don't just adlib endlessly

Chapter Three – Articulation

In the chapters that follow, we'll begin to look at bassline ideas we can play over the most common chord progressions in jazz-funk. But, before we do, let's dig a little deeper into the topic of articulation. Perhaps it *doesn't* go without saying that it's not just about the notes we play – *how* we play them is everything!

So, in this chapter, we'll work through some exercises to help you develop my favourite types of articulation. Using these techniques is the key to highlighting notes and phrases that will add character and personality to your playing. They will also separate a mediocre bassline from a great one. Enjoy experimenting with these techniques and finding where you can embellish your playing.

Slides

As well as the classic big bass slides that are often used to transition into a new section of a tune, slides can be very effective when used in phrases. Sliding into, or slurring notes, rather than playing everything straight is an immediate attention grabber.

In bar one of Example 3a, the bassline uses only two notes, E and D, but adding slides immediately turns it into a more interesting phrase. Here, I'm using ascending and descending slides to highlight the movement.

In bars two and four, slide from F# to G on the A string with the first finger. Then, while keeping the lower octave G in place, play the G to F# slide on the G string with the third finger. Holding the lower octave while playing notes above it is an idea I use a lot to glue a bassline together.

Example 3a

Hammer-ons

Hammer-ons are a commonly used bass articulation technique, especially when players are slapping using pentatonic scale patterns.

To be more individual, try mixing up the timing and use the character of the hammer-on as part of your phrase.

Here, after playing a solid downbeat at the beginning of bar one, playing the next phrase on the "&" of beat 2 makes the line much less predictable. Including a hammer-on here makes the phrase sound smoother and more fluid. This idea then becomes a motif for the rest of the bassline.

Notice that we omit the strong downbeat at the beginning of bar two and just leave space. It's a dotted 1/8th note rest, so listen to the audio to really capture the timing and feel. Notice also that the notes are all taken from the E Minor Pentatonic scale and played in four-note cellular phrases.

Example 3b

Pull-offs

Next, here is an example of how pull-offs and hammer-ons can be combined to add character to how the bassline is presented.

The phrase in bars two and four would sound quite different if it was played straight, with every note plucked without articulation.

Here, we use the idea of plucking a note, then playing the same note as part of a pull-off phrase, then we play an adjacent note and repeat *that* note as part of a hammer-on. The overall effect is a much more fluid line.

Timing is key here, so that the phrasing doesn't sound loose. It's very easy to let your timing slip when using hammer-ons/pull-offs, so focus on keeping the bassline tight and grooving.

Example 3c

Trills & "Funk Vibrato"

A trill is a fast hammer-on and pull-off action that is repeated and is a nice way to embellish a note. It's a great technique that you'll hear used a lot in soul, RnB, and funk, but it perhaps doesn't have as much attitude as the "funk vibrato" or "sizzle" (or whatever you'd like to call it!)

The idea here is to move your finger back and forth over a fret to create a fast, wide vibrato. As soon as you hear it, you'll understand what I mean, and I've no doubt you'll have heard it on countless funk recordings. Both techniques are great ways to finish a short phrase and add some character.

The difference is subtle but noticeable. I tend to use a trill for a "neater" sound and a sizzle for more attitude. In bars 3-4 here the "tr" is played as a sizzle.

Example 3d

Combining Techniques

Now let's look at some examples where we combine these techniques to create some advanced, articulated basslines.

First, a line that uses slaps and pops with hammer-ons and pull-offs.

We're in the key of B Minor and the progression starts with the v chord (F#m7).

The line begins with a movement from the b7 (E) to the root (F#), which is then repeated in the higher octave. This is followed by some dead note articulation, then a movement from the 4th (B) to the 5th (C#) of the chord. The note choices are fairly simple, so this line is all about the articulation, focusing on the percussive effect of the slaps and pops to form a melodic bassline.

In bars 3-4 we keep the same idea going over the VI chord (Gmaj7) and move to the tonic chord in bars 5-6.

By bar six it feels right to open things up a little more and play a fill. The fill phrase uses more colourful note choices, drawing from the parent scale rather than thinking about chord tones, and a C# note is used a couple of times, which implies a Bm9 harmony.

The timing of this phrase is as important as the articulation being used, so be sure to compare what you're playing with the audio example to nail down those staccato 1/8th notes followed by 1/16th note rests.

The line ends in bar eight with a fast fill phrase that includes a chromatic note (G#), which creates some surprise and tension as the bassline turns around.

Example 3e

Next up is a line I dubbed "Louis Graham", characteristic of the styles of funk legends Larry Graham and Louis Johnson. Both were capable of producing incredible driving bass parts that became the main feature of their tunes. Check out *Pow* by Larry Graham and Graham Central Station, and *Streetwave* by The Brothers Johnson. Also take a listen to Louis Johnson's hypnotic bassline on the track *Get on the Floor* by Michael Jackson from his classic album *Off the Wall*.

This is a busy, Pow-style line that is constantly moving and designed to be the hook of the tune. It features extensive use of hammer-ons and pull-offs, which are slapped and popped accordingly, and the result is a slippery, driving line.

This bassline works over an Em7 vamp, but rather than use the straight E Minor scale, I opted for the more sophisticated sounding E Dorian scale to inform the note choices. E Dorian contains notes identical to E Natural Minor, apart from the 6th degree.

Where E Natural Minor has a b6 (C), E Dorian has a natural 6th (C#), and it's this note that gives the Dorian its characterful cool vibe.

I suggest working through this line slowly, bar-by-bar, to first get to grips with the timing of the groove. You can think of bar one as a series of 1/16th notes that fill the bar, but we omit the very first note for a 1/16th note rest. The E note at the end of bar one is tied, so that it crosses the bar line and occupies the first 1/16th note of bar two.

At the end of bar two, the D note on the top string is popped, then we slide from the 7th to 9th frets to play the E, held for an 1/8th note, before we drop the low E to hang over the bar line again.

In the even numbered bars you'll find other variations of this idea to create fills. It's like a "question and answer" part, where the "question" (odd numbered bars) remains the same throughout and is answered in different ways.

Example 3f

Here is a line with some tricky articulation for you to work on. It uses hammer-ons, pull-offs and slides, but also includes some wide string skips and occasional harmonics.

This line works well over an Em6 vamp. The Em6 chord contains a C# note, so the E Dorian scale with its natural 6th is the perfect fit here. Slow this line down to begin with and work out your fingering movements. Then, when you're comfortable navigating the string skips, add in the articulation to give the line its distinctive character.

Example 3g

To end the chapter, this final example was played freely as an improvisation, and I had in mind to capture the flavour of wine!

It shows how a simple triad phrase can be embellished with some slides, harmonics and, of course, some space. The line starts with an E minor triad climbing up to the octave, then targeting the 9th (F#) but embellishing that note with a quick ascending 1/32nd note slide into the 10th (G) and back, before resolving to the root note.

The addition of harmonics brings some chordal tension to what is essentially a groove in E Minor. The first harmonics chord on beat 4 of bar one is an F6, and the harmonics sound the pitches of A and D. I slide the low note from E to F. Play the low notes with the second finger of the fretting hand and the harmonics will fall nicely for the first finger.

Note that an F6 chord can also be viewed as an inversion of Dm, so this sound just adds some tension and movement away from the tonal centre of E minor for a beat.

In a similar fashion, bar two features the same movement two frets lower. This results in an Ebmaj7 chord as the harmonics sound the pitches of D and G. It could also be viewed as an Em7 where the bass note is lowered a half step to create more tension and interest.

Bar four ends with harmonics playing F# and B notes, which give the effect of a passing chord before the idea repeats.

At the very end, we finish the idea with the top notes of an Em6/9 chord, but without its root note – just for a bit of intrigue!

Example 3h

Chapter Four – Minor Chord Vamp Ideas

One of the staple elements of the funk music genre is the "vamp". This is the idea of grooving on just a single chord for an extended period of time and there are hundreds of examples out there. Mostly, vamps will use either minor chords, dominant 7 chords, or a combination of both (such as a repeating ii – V progression e.g., Em7 – A7). In the next few chapters we'll cover all these scenarios, beginning with minor chords.

Playing over just one chord sounds easy in theory, but actually it's a challenge. We can quickly run out of ideas and start to sound boring, so we need to get creative with it.

When considering what to play over a vamp, we need to apply the tools we've discussed in the previous three chapters:

- **Focus on rhythm first.** Think about note placement and controlling note length. Remember that adding effective syncopation is the key to bringing the funk to any idea

- **Use simple motifs** as a way to generate melodic ideas. Motif-based ideas can give our basslines a core theme and glue together every idea

- **Add articulation for character**. With the previous essential elements in place, we can get more creative with our basslines and add personality using legato slides, hammer-ons and pull-offs, trills and funk vibrato

- **Also, never forget about using space**. Even when a part is established, excitement can be created by dropping out expected notes and leaving the space!

In the following examples, I'll show you how I try to find catchy themes, combining rhythm and note choice, to create basslines that are memorable but still supportive to the rest of the band or the other elements of the arrangement.

I'll stretch out these basslines to two- or four-bar phrases before they repeat, and you can loop them around for longer when you practice to the drum track.

Before we get into the examples, however, let me introduce a new tool for you to add to your bassline generation options. All of these lines can be played over a static Em7 chord, but a great way to create new material is to *imply* chord changes that are not written.

In other words, we imagine that there are additional chord changes in the tune we're playing, then spell them out with our bassline. For example, in the next couple of lines, the note choices and the order in which those notes are played suggest that the chord progression could be Em7 – Gmaj7 – F#m7.

The concept of *implied changes* is one that is used extensively in jazz and lends itself well to the extended vamp scenarios of funk.

In this first example, we only play on the downbeat on beat 1 of bar one. In the subsequent three bars, the opening notes are anticipated with a 1/16th note. So, the G note that you'd expect to hear at the start of bar two, for example, is brought forward to the end of bar one and played as a 1/16th note. The result is that it sounds just before beat 1 of bar two. This idea is often referred to as a *push*.

This bassline is essentially a four-bar idea that is repeated, but I introduced a couple of slight variations, so listen carefully to the audio.

Example 4a

This next example takes the motif idea of the previous line and shows how it can be developed. Harmonically, the note choices are very similar, but here we add some scale and chromatic approaches and a hammer-on phrase. These 1/16th note chromatic passing notes are so important to perfect in your playing, as they feature in many great basslines, and a wealth of phrases specific to the jazz-funk genre can be generated using them.

Example 4b

Example 4c ups the rhythmic complexity with a busier variation that is highly syncopated. Although this is a more complicated approach on the face of it, we can clearly trace back the roots of this idea to the original, simpler motif.

Keep in mind our implied chord changes to spice up the bassline: Em7 – G – F#m. This time I'm also thinking of a passing Bm chord before the repeat. Although we mustn't forget that, in reality, we're just playing over a static Em7 vamp, I've written the implied changes in the notation for this example to help you visualise how the bassline is constructed.

If you think of each of these chords as *target root notes* (E, G, F#, B), then you'll see that the 1/16th note variations and embellishments that have been added are all set in place to approach these target notes. The only exception to this is at the end of bar three, where a B note is targeted chromatically from below. Here I was simply aiming for the 3rd of the G major chord in my imaginary progression.

In bar two I added one of my favourite ideas, which is to play an ascending slide or hammer-on, followed by a descending slide. Slide into the low G from below, then play the descending slide from the G octave to F# to create a nice articulation in the phrasing.

Finally, in bars 7-8 I add some excitement with a mixture of descending chromatics, hammer-ons and a 1/16th note *push* – this time with the E Minor Pentatonic scale in mind.

Example 4c

Now let's move on and look at some other vamp ideas. This line works over an Am9 vamp. You could also throw in a whole step movement to a Bm11 chord on the last two beats of bars two and four.

Play this line using palm muting throughout to deaden the strings and loop it around, playing along with the audio to nail down the groove.

Example 4d

Let's change key again, this time to D Minor. Here's a line based around the D Minor Pentatonic scale (D, F, G, A, C) that uses a combination of techniques over a medium-fast-paced straight funk groove.

To create some funky separation between the drums and bass in bar one, the first two notes are played on the off-beats, allowing the kick drum, then the snare, to be heard on their own. In the latter half of the bar we change tack and drop Dm7 chord tones (the b3 then the root) on the downbeats to play with the kick and snare. This "off-beat followed by downbeat" syncopation adds lots of groove and urgency to the line.

Example 4e

Here is a simple two-bar line over an A minor to E minor harmony. In bar two, the popped note is played on the off-beat, so that the kick and snare can be heard on either side of it. It's another example of working with the drum groove to create syncopation, rather than slavishly following the bass drum.

Example 4f

In the next example, we play a simple two-bar line over a G minor groove. We're using the G Dorian scale to compose the line, and the idea here is to outline the harmony using a few intervallic leaps. The natural 6th of the Dorian scale makes an appearance here, so a Gm6 is an appropriate backing chord.

In bar one, we string skip from a low G root note to the b7 (F) of Gm6. Then we move from the 5th (D) to the natural 6th (E) and down to the b3 (Bb). I hope you'll agree that dropping the b3 on a downbeat here is a cool sound that's not often used.

In bar two we highlight the b7 as a way of creating a tension that wants to resolve back to the root of the chord.

In bars four and eight, we highlight the natural 6th again with a wide string skip.

Example 4g

For the final example in this chapter I turned to my upright bass and wrote out a funky practice etude in D Minor for you to take into your practice sessions. Yes, it's possible to be funky on upright bass too, as players like Chris Minh Doky, Christian McBride, and trailblazers like Cecil McBee have proven, and the fretless nature of the instrument makes expressive slides easy to execute. Work through it carefully, then play along with me on the audio.

Example 4h

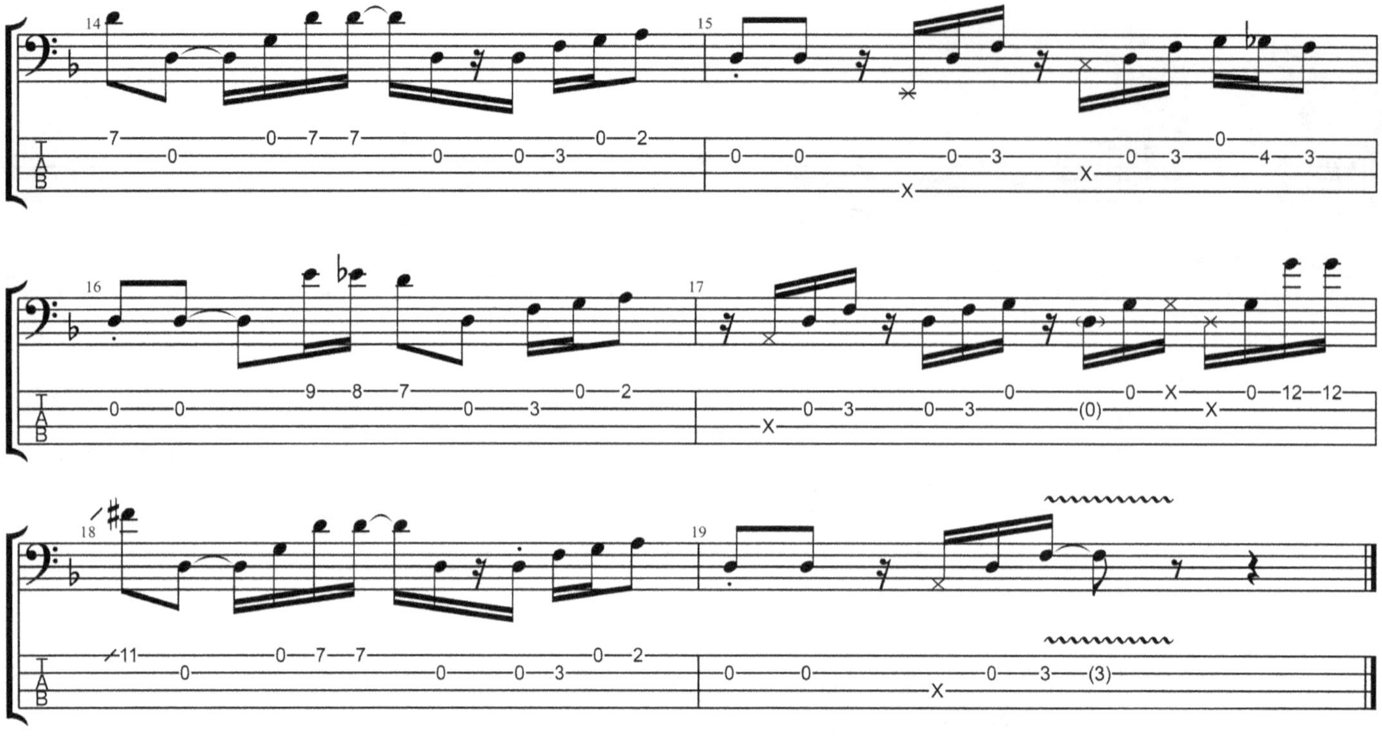

Chapter Five – Dominant Chord Vamp Ideas

Let's continue to develop our use of articulation to add some character and flavour to our basslines. In this chapter, we'll look at how to create some funky parts that suit dominant 7 chords and vamps – a common harmonic structure in the jazz-funk genre.

The examples here are played over a static A7 chord. In order to highlight the sound of this dominant 7, we can reference its chord tones (A, C#, E, G) but at the same time, we don't need to be fixated with them – it's cool to add some interest with other notes too – and dominant 7 chords will take "tension" notes better than any other chord type.

We'll draw some of our ideas from the A Mixolydian scale. This is the fifth mode of the D Major scale, but in practical terms it makes more sense to compare it to the A Major scale.

A Major has the scale formula: 1 2 3 4 5 6 7 (A, B, C#, D, E, F#, G#)

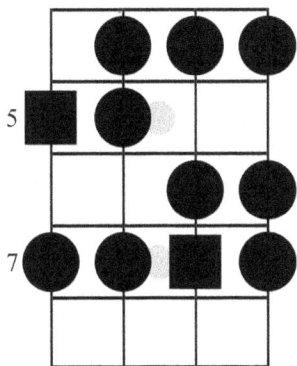

A Mixolydian has the scale formula: 1 2 3 4 5 6 b7 (A, B, C#, D, E, F#, G)

In other words, it's just like playing an A Major scale with a b7 (G) rather than a natural 7th (G#). Since you probably know your major scale inside out, you only have to think about relocating one note, and pay attention to how that change affects the patterns you play.

Compare the 5th position patterns for A Major and A Mixolydian below. A Mixolydian scale tones are shown as hollow circles around A Major scale tones on the right-hand diagram.

A Major Scale   A Mixolydian Scale

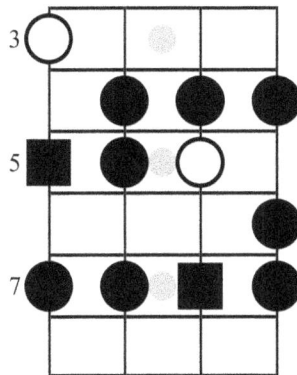

If we start by laying down a simple rhythm with a root note approach, then any decoration we add around it will be very noticeable.

To begin with, using A (root), G (b7) and E (5th) notes, keeps the line moving without drawing too much attention. The F# note from A Mixolydian in bar 4 adds a little more flavour. When played over an A7 chord, F# is the 13th interval.

Some decoration in bar eight stretches out the part even more. The use of D and C natural notes leading into the C# (3rd of A7) adds some tension and act like an "enclosure" of the target chord tone. Bouncing between F# and G notes over the A7 is also a cool sound.

Example 5a

In the next example, you should be able to hear the connection with the previous idea. Here we are using similar note choices and methods of targeting the chord tones and decorating the notes, so the theoretical explanation is the same.

However, this is a much busier line, driven by its syncopation. We could combine ideas like 5a and 5b to provide two distinct but connected parts for different sections of a song, depending on how much space is being left by the other instruments.

Example 5b

Next, a line with more demanding articulation, which moves away from beginning on a root note.

Although many bass players teach students to always lock in with the bass drum, we don't have to follow this idea religiously. Often it is effective to do so, but it's equally effective not to, and it can be more dramatic to allow a kick drum beat to cut through the mix on its own.

We don't always have to play on beat 1 of the bar either. If the drums are strong on the downbeat, the bass can "bounce" off it instead.

The line in bar one is a slippery legato phrase that begins on the "& of beat 1 with a hammer-on figure, which moves into a pedal tone idea, where D and C# notes on the top string are played against a G pedal tone.

In the latter half of bar one, I play a variation of my favourite "Turner-ism": the ascending slide followed by a descending slide, or in this case, a pull-off.

Notice in bars two and four that the line is grounded with strong notes placed on beats 2 and 4.

Example 5c

Here is a slippery, off-beat syncopated A7 groove with some sliding articulation.

Timing and accuracy are everything with this line, because it's easy to play a bassline like this loosely when it needs to be super tight.

Rhythmically, it's a mix of 1/16th and 1/8th notes and the note placement is very important in maintaining the groove.

To learn it, slow things down and count bar one in 1/16th notes:

"1-e-&-a, 2-e-&-a, 3-e-&-a, 4-e-&-a"

After a 1/16th note rest, the first two notes in bar one are played on the "e" and "&" of beat 1.

The next two notes fall on the "e" and "&" of beat 2.

Then, a dotted 1/8th note rest means that the next note falls on the "a" of beat 3. This is immediately followed by a note on the "1" of beat 4, played as a staccato 1/8th note, leading into the end of the phrase.

Because we tend to be creatures of habit, we like being able to identify a pattern and fall in line with it, but the syncopations here are a purposely unpredictable to create more interest!

The rhythm remains similar throughout, so once you've mastered bar one, you can apply that rhythm to the other bars.

Example 5d

Chapter Six – Two-Chord Vamp Ideas

Now we turn our attention to another common jazz-funk harmony: the two-chord vamp. Often, these will be ii – V movements, effectively combining the minor 7 and dominant 7 chords we've looked at.

The ii – V cadence is such a strong, common sound in all forms of music that it will serve any bass player well to have multiple ideas for playing over it.

However, it's also common in jazz-funk to have other two-chord movements – ones based on different interval jumps, or with a more modal feel, so we'll explore that too.

In this chapter I want to highlight a strategy that I feel is a cool approach to playing over two-chord vamps. As much as we should try to find common tones when playing over changes to make a seamless switch between chords, it's great to be able to highlight their differences. If we can include some of the *strong* notes from a chord change, this can add tension and interest to our bassline.

We'll start with two chords that are *not* a ii – V movement: Em9 to G9. These extended five-note chords share three notes in common, and both have two notes different from each other.

Em9: E, G, B, D, F#

G9: G, B, D, F, A

Understanding this presents us with the "safe" and the more "interesting" notes choices.

G, B and D are the shared notes we could use if we were looking for a "safe" way to move between chords. The other tones are less obvious choices.

I use an F note in bars two and six to highlight the G9 (its b7) and also to signal the change in harmony. If the chord was still Em9 we'd expect to hear an F# rather than an F. This adds an unexpected quality to the line.

By contrast, in bars four and eight, I opt for the shared B note to highlight the 3rd of the G9 chord.

Other characteristics of this line are bouncing off the downbeats in bars one, two and three, and lots of syncopation throughout.

In bar eight I add some variation to the line with popped accents (even popping on the A string for a funky tone). Adding a variation like this just before the line loops around, stretches out the idea and makes it feel longer before it repeats.

Example 6a

Let's change the chord progression and move to a ii – V movement between Am9 and D9 chords.

NB: the audio for this example was played on a five-string bass for a fat bottom end sound, but is notated here in Drop D tuning to keep it within the four-string bass format. Tune your E string down a whole step to D to play this example.

This time we do play the downbeats, but we still keep a "bounce" note by playing an off-beat 1/16th note in the lower octave. Playing so many root notes with a strong rhythm really drives this part.

For articulation, I used fast slides in bars two and four. In bar two, a tip here is to fret the slide with the first finger to get you in position for bar three.

Bar four uses a fill constructed from D9 chord tones (D, F#, A, C, E). In bar eight, the same lick is played but expanded on. The last phrase of the bar moves away from the chord tone approach to play a bluesy lick with the A Blues scale, just focusing on the overall A Minor tonality.

Play this line with very staccato short notes and use palm muting throughout.

Example 6b

Let's change the harmony again, this time to a ii – V movement played in reverse (G7 – Dm7).

Rhythmically, this is quite a classic jazz-funk syncopation that you may have heard before, but it's good to have these ideas in your musical arsenal.

The use of chromatic notes to walk up to chord changes is also classic jazz-funk. Here, we are highlighting those go-to funky notes of the 3rd and b7. Again, the notes are played staccato here, so be sure to nail the rhythm and feel.

Example 6c

I thought it would be fun to show how the classic style of Example 6c can be embellished. We have the same chord changes and similar note choices with chromatic approaches, but I've added some approach notes to lead into the B note (3rd of G7) in bar one, each time it occurs.

Check out the E note at the end of bar one that follows the chromatic walk up. It's a lead-in note targeting the root note of the Dm7 at the beginning of bar two, approaching it from a whole step above.

At the end of bars two and four, this line uses a deliberately "out" note to add some tension and bring on the "bass face"! We have a Bb where the chord tone would an A note. It's great to throw in the occasional surprise note for effect, and it can quickly be resolved as we move to the next bar. The first time this idea is played, I add some funk vibrato too.

Example 6d

OK, now it's time for a slapped idea! However, this bassline could be played with fingers, pick, even using palm-muting if you like, and still sound funky.

The reason I chose to slap this line was to encourage some movement away from using only octave patterns or fast rhythms over single notes when slapping.

Feel free to experiment with this idea and explore using the slaps, pops and hammer-ons to alter its character and phrasing.

Note that this two-bar loop is repeated almost identically, except for the two 1/16th notes in bar four. Again, we're bringing in a small variation to extend our loop.

Example 6e

Here's a different idea over similar chord changes.

Here, I'm breaking up the sound of funky octaves with the distinctive interval of an Em6 chord: it's C# note. Notice that it adds a certain quirkiness to the idea.

The interest in this bassline also comes from the idea of ascending notes on the G string.

First, we have the C# from the minor 6 chord. Then, it's a D note over the A9 chord in bar two. (The D is an extended tone that implies the sound of A11). For the A13 chord in the latter half of bar two, it's an E note (the 5th). Finally, the F# note at the 11th fret implies we're playing over an Em9 chord.

You can have a lot of fun playing with ideas like this and even impose limits on yourself, such as trying the opposite of this idea – finding chord tones that are descending on one string, for instance.

Example 6f

Next, we're changing to a Gm7 to C9, ii – V sequence.

This idea is all about trying to give a bouncing feel that still feels rhythmically grounded. The notes come from the G Natural Minor scale (G, A, Bb, C, D, Eb, F).

I play a lot of fills like the one in bars four and eight. The 4th intervals in this lick give it a modern, funky sound. When practicing this line to tempo, focus on getting the groove sounding tight with accurate note placement.

Example 6g

Playing around the downbeat and aiming for catchy rhythms and note choices tends to make for strong hooks – basslines that are inseparable from the song, not just supporting it.

Notice that in all the odd numbered bars in this idea where we're focusing on the G root note, no notes are played on *any* of the downbeats. This means that every kick and snare hit is clearly heard, while the bass fits around them, giving clear separation and making the whole sound ever so funky.

If we count this bar as 1/16th notes, then the accents fall as below (highlighted in bold type):

"1 **e & ** a, 2 e **&** **a**, 3 e & a, 4 **e & a**."

Viewed like this, you can see that no beat in the bar is treated the same, with the 1/16th note placement shifting each time.

Play this one through slowly a few times to nail the rhythms before bringing it up to tempo.

Example 6h

It's often worth trying the same ideas using different techniques, so here is the same line but this time we're slapping it.

Try using a rootsy tone for this idea, rather than going for a high-fidelity, refined sound. Tone is very personal and we all like to hear different things, but I suggest exploring this idea, as it can give a line like this real personality.

Example 6i

Auditioning Bassline Ideas

To end this chapter we're going to play over a soul-funk groove, and we'll "audition" three different bassline ideas.

Each idea is quite distinct, and what I want you to take from this is the fact that there are many routes we can take when creating basslines. Testing out different ideas and auditioning them is a great way of discovering *the* bassline that really fits the tune. It can also be a way of creating multiple versions of a bassline for different sections of a song.

We'll start out really simple, with a heavily grooving part that is played over the chord changes Em7 – Am7 – Bm7.

Example 6j

Based on the same chord changes, here is a much busier, syncopated part.

It features a catchy motif with a repeated note that appears in the latter half of each bar, starting on beat 3.

Here, the idea is that the motif remains almost entirely the same (apart from one note) while the chords change underneath it. In bar one, the notes of the motif represent the b3 (G), 9th (F#) and b7 (D) of an Em9 chord.

The next time it occurs it is played over a Bm7 chord. This time, the end of the motif changes slightly and morphs into another idea. Over Bm7 the G note is dissonant (implying a Bm7b13 tonality), but because the rhythm remains the same and the motif is a strong phrase, our ears accept this momentary tension.

Example 6k

Adding articulation to embellish a bassline can really breathe life into it and transform it. In this variation of the bassline, prominent hammer-on/pull-off embellishments feature in every bar. It's easy to play this kind of figure a little sloppily if we're not careful, so work at getting the legato phrases sounding really slick.

Example 6l

Here are all three ideas combined into a longer practice etude. You'll hear that I add some slight variations to the three main themes, and also add a few fills to make the transitions between them as seamless as possible.

I've also changed the order in which the lines appear. Rather than starting simple and gradually getting more complicated, I've used the first simple idea later on as a kind of breakdown.

Try and learn the whole etude off by heart, then continue jamming with the drum backing track to invent your own variations and create new ideas.

Example 6m

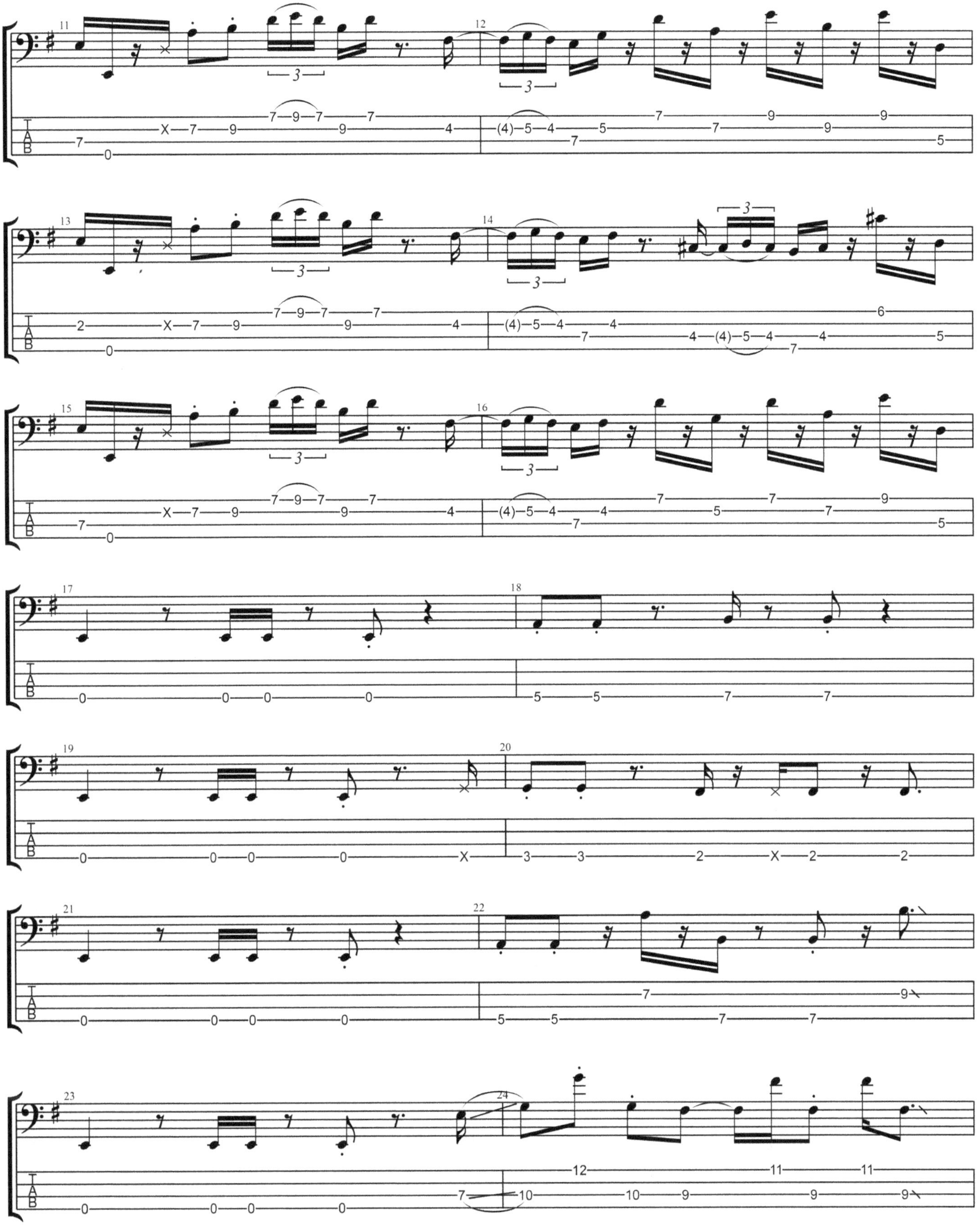

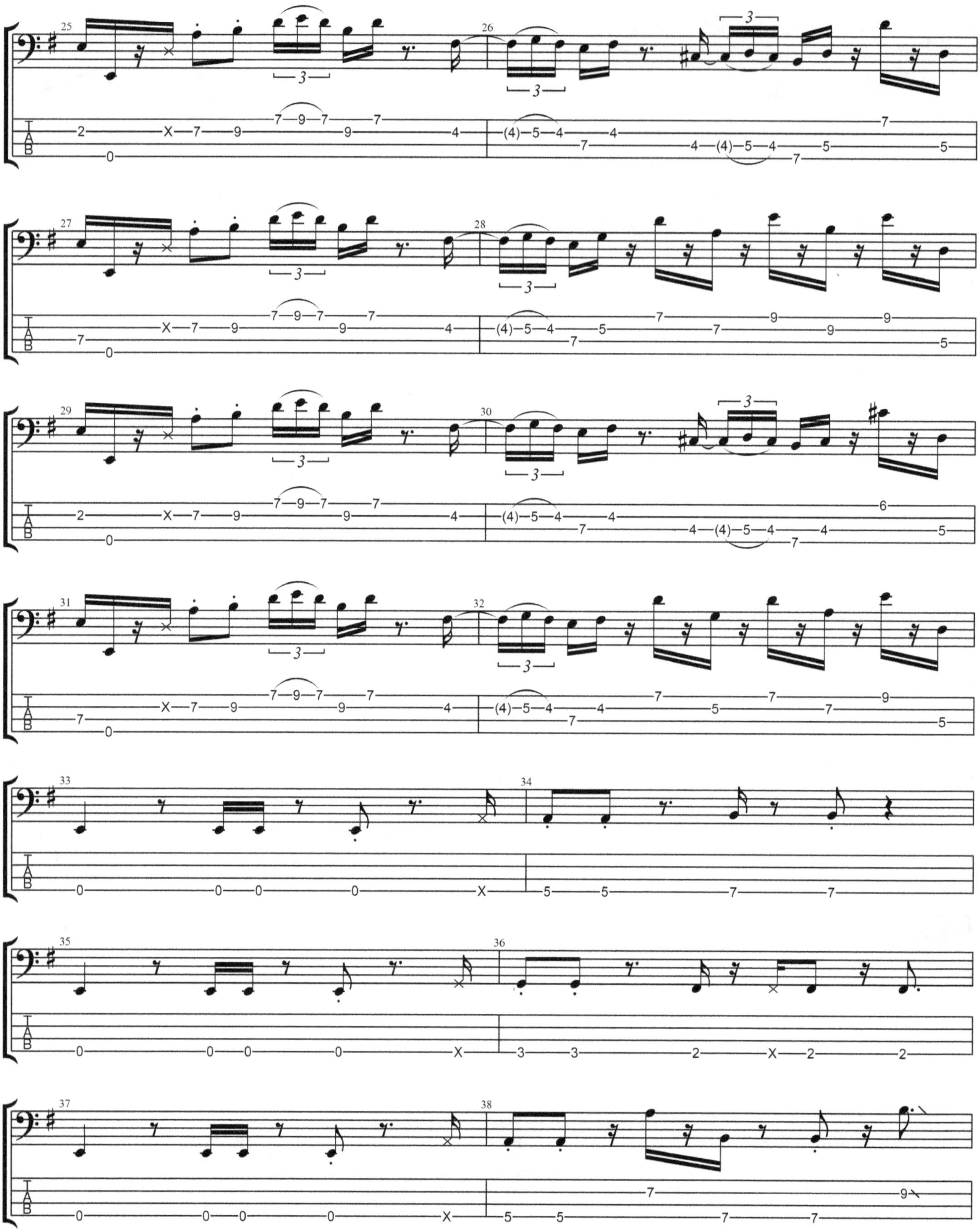

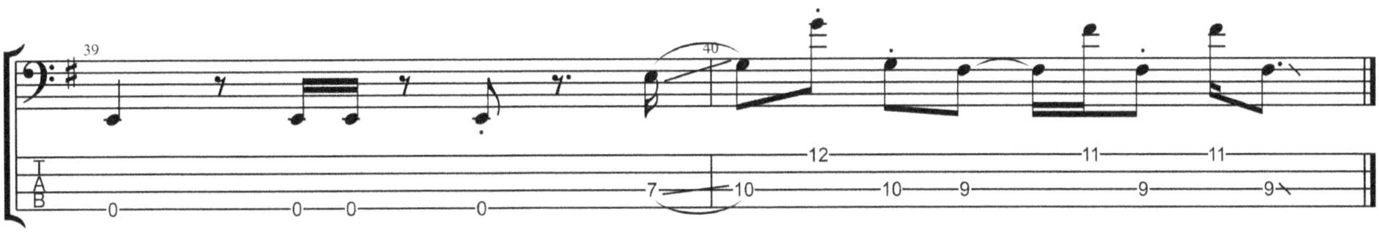
39
40

Chapter Seven – Creating Basslines Over Longer Chord Sequences

Not all tunes in jazz-funk are based around vamps, of course, and some have complex chord changes, so in this chapter we'll look at a series of ideas for playing over longer/more involved chord progressions.

This first example of constructing a line to flow through a set of chord changes shows that the use of rhythmic and harmonic ideas can be stretched beyond simply repeating an idea for every change. While we keep the exact same motif for all the odd-numbered bars, the motif in the even-numbered bars is varied each time. In bar eight, lots of embellishment is added, so that we have effectively created an eight-bar bassline.

The aim of the rhythm and note choices is to keep the line catchy by using similar phrasing, but also to make it interesting via the variations.

I have used the occasional slide, hammer-on and even a pop to add character and vary the timbre of the line. The very last phrase is a pedal-tone idea that bounces off the open A string.

Example 7a

We used this bassline earlier, but it lends itself to a richer harmony, so here we are repurposing it to create a cool new idea.

Example 7b

Here is an example of how a strong rhythmic motif can be used to travel through a set of changes. Again, I've tried to stretch out the repeat here, this time by using a two-bar rhythmic phrase over bars 1-2, then repeating a one-bar phrase that feels like a hook.

The two-bar phrase from bars 1-2 is repeated in bars 5-6, but over a slightly different harmony. The line that works so well over Gmaj9 also works over Cmaj9, but now the notes represent different intervals.

The same happens with the one-bar phrase stated in bar three, then repeated in bar four, but with different chord changes. The note choices highlight different intervals over the "new" chords in bar four and alter the mood of the line accordingly.

Example 7c

Next, here's a funky idea that spells out a IV – iii – ii progression in the key of A Major.

This kind of sequence is typical in jazz-funk, where the chords have momentum and are heading somewhere, but never actually resolve to the tonic chord of the key, so that the real key centre is somewhat disguised.

This line uses the simple strategy of targeting the root notes of the chords. However, apart from the Dmaj7 chord, the root notes are played on off-beats, to work around the kick drum rather than play with it.

The overall effect is to increase the momentum and urgency of the groove. Make sure to add the heavy articulation at the end of each two-bar loop.

Example 7d

Now try this fast, club-style bouncing bassline that works over a i – v – iv progression in the key of A Minor.

The main feature of this idea is the syncopated two-bar hook played over the Am chord in bars 1-2. To achieve the catchy hook we're combining a few ideas.

First, to achieve the "bounce" we're using the technique of playing a dead note, followed by repeating notes. The repeating notes are F#s (a chromatic note, not found in the key of A Minor) which resolve to the G chord tone, the b7 of A minor. This is using the Dorian scale (natural 6th to flat 7) and adds a bit of tension to the line.

Second, the C note played at the end of bars 1-2 is played as a dotted 1/8th note on the "e" of beat 4. I.e., we are splitting beat 4 into four 1/16th notes ("4-e-&-a") and dropping the note immediately after beat 4, so that it floats over the bar line.

A similar thing happens in bar three, where we anticipate the root of the D minor chord that occurs in bar four by playing it the "& of beat 4 in bar three.

Example 7e

The next example follows a funky theme, playing over more complex changes in Drop D tuning. It's predominantly an 1/8th note idea with 1/16th note accents and fills, and the use of occasional slides and ghost notes to outline movement in an overall tonal centre of G Minor.

A strong rhythmic character is established by repeating the bassline movement every four bars and using disciplined note length. The space is essential in this type of bassline, and the use of octaves and 1/8th note walks helps to highlight the notes they lead into.

Example 7f

E♭maj7   E♭maj7   A♭13

B♭/C   Fmaj9   Fsus13

E♭maj7   Gm   D7♭9

Here's bassline over a darker chord progression that moves between Em7 and Fmaj7.

In bar one, we begin on the low root note, then jump up to the minor 10th (the b3 of the chord moved up an octave). Then we play the b7 of the chord (D) to lead back into the octave root note.

In bar two, although the Fmaj7 chord has a major 3rd (A), to create some tension I played what sounds like an F Major Pentatonic phrase but with a b3 (Ab). It's a quick, passing note, but it's enough to catch the listener's attention with a moment of surprise.

If the phrase in bar two is the "question", then the answer comes in bar four where we walk chromatically up to the major 3rd (A).

To retain the darker vibe of the bassline, in bar five the note choices come from the E Dorian scale. This is identical to the E Minor scale except that it has a major 6th (C#) rather than a b6 (C). The movement from G to C# (minor 10th to 6th) creates a dissonant tritone before playing D to E (b7 to octave).

The two notes at the end of bar six anticipate the change back to Em7 in bar seven. Then, at the end of bar eight there is a classic funk ascending/descending slide in the upper register. These notes may sound random but they create specific tensions over the Fmaj7 chord. The Gb is the b9, and the B note is the #11 – both very tense sounds over Fmaj7 to provide another moment of surprise.

Example 7g

By constructing a bassline around a more exotic scale we can create a less common chord sequence and also have a set of interesting leading tones at our fingertips to create some nice tensions.

This idea uses the E Half-Whole Diminished scale. It's an octatonic scale, which means it consists of eight pitches rather than the usual seven (like all major and minor scales). The scale has the notes: E, F, G, G#, Bb, B, C#, D.

Contained within those scale tones are the notes of four minor 7 chords:

- Em7: E, G, B, D
- C#m7: C#, E, G#, B
- Gm7: G, Bb, D, F
- Bbm7: Bb, Db (C#), F, Ab (G#)

We'll use the first three of those chords to form our progression.

This bassline is played using an envelope filter to create an even more distinctive part. While many funk tunes have a more comfortable sound, I think it's cool to have some darker intervals and some unexpected twists.

This can also set the foundation for a more jazz-orientated melody, and that's how I think of this line. We're using the chord tones of Em7, C#m7 and Gm7, but we're utilising the other notes in the scale which, in context, sound like chromatic approach or passing notes.

All the notes come from E Half-Whole Diminished apart from one additional chromatic note, the Gb that is part of the descending walk down at the end of every four bars.

The overall feel you're aiming for here is "staccato snappy" and if you have an envelope filter pedal it's worth using it for this line as it really helps achieve that effect.

Example 7h

In the next example we're using the upper register to create a signature bassline. This is also played with an envelope filter and I'm outlining the chords with some colourful notes.

In bar one, the notes of the bassline come from superimposing an Am7 over the Dm7 harmony, which creates a rich, Dm(sus9) sound. An arpeggio over the Bbmaj7 chord in bar two starts on the major 7th then hammers onto the root.

To outline the Ebmaj7 chord, I played a Bb and a high G (the 5th and the 10th), but the sound of the 6th interval together is one of my favourite sounds (like a B6).

On beat four of the Ebmaj7 I play a bebop-style phrase using the 7th and 5th (D and Bb), then play the same intervals but descend chromatically to hit the C root note at the beginning of bar four.

Note the use of different note lengths throughout this line, with a mix of longer held notes and fast phrases. In terms of the tone, I chose to set the envelope filter (a vintage Mutron) to almost overload with resonance. The use of dynamics, phrasing and tone are all personal preferences. This is what appeals to me, but you need to discover what most appeals to you!

Example 7i

Next, here is a small variation on this line, adding an embellishment at the end of bar two with an additional hammer-on.

Example 7j

Here is one more subtle variation on this theme. In bar three, we're targeting the Db note on beat "4&" via a different route. To make bar four of the bassline funkier, we're adding some dead note articulation.

Example 7k

To end this chapter, here's one more idea over a different chord sequence.

This time, we're playing over a i – VI – v progression in the key of E Minor. This is an example of how we can stretch what is essentially a two-bar idea to eight bars.

You'll notice that the line played over the E minor bars remains the same throughout. Then, the line over Cmaj7 and Bm7 is the same in bars three and seven only. In bars five and nine we are playing different fills over these chords, so that we can extend the idea and create the overall effect that this line is heading somewhere.

My strategy when playing basslines like this is to try and acknowledge the chord tones, at the same time adding some colour using extended notes or scale tones. For example, I use the 9th and the 4th/11th in the opening phrase alongside the expected b7. The tonal centre is E Minor, so I can use E minor themed scales for the fills, even over the Bm7 chord.

I opted to draw from the E Blues scale. In bar four I use this scale to play an ascending line. Then, in bar eight, I play a bluesy lick with a quick slide up to the "blue note" (Bb) and back to the A. You'll no doubt be familiar with this type of lick in guitar playing, but here I choose to play an E minor type lick over the Bm7 chord for a different vibe.

Example 71

Chapter Eight – Final Study Piece

To conclude our exploration of funky bass I want us to look together at a longer study piece. Here we have a complete tune of almost 5 minutes in length with a few repeating sections, and our task is to compose a compelling bassline that will not only integrate with the existing keys and guitar parts, but be a feature of the song.

I'll show you what I came up with, and we'll discuss that, but then it's over to you to jam over the backing track, compose and edit your ideas, and create your own bassline.

As we work through the tune and break down the ideas, you'll see a recurring theme. These are good rules for composing any bassline:

- Start with the seed of an idea

- Repeat it

- Embellish/decorate it with appropriate fills

- Experiment with your articulation

In some respects, it's easier to come up with a good riff over a short vamp than it is to conceive a bassline for a whole song, but the above stages will help with the editing process.

In the first instance, we need to come up with a riff or phrase that fits with the harmony, is not too busy, and bears repeating.

This idea initially came from my intention to show that a funk bassline doesn't always have to start on a downbeat, especially beat 1 of bar one. The playing of some of my funk bass heroes might imply that's exactly what we *should* do – and that definitely has its place – but remember it's the interaction between the instruments that makes a piece of music funky. So, for us bassists, it's all about how we use syncopation, placing certain notes on downbeats and others on off-beats.

We're going to pull out the main sections of this tune and examine them. At the end of the chapter, you have the TAB/notation for the entire tune.

Example 8a shows the seed of the idea and, right from the start, the riff misses beat 1 and "bounces" off the downbeat. We have a 1/16th note rest at the beginning of the bar, but that's followed by a dotted 1/8th note, which gives the bassline a strong start and allows that first note to float over the beat. The open E string placed just before beat 3 of bar one also adds some bounce to the line.

Another feature here is the "pushed" feel at the end of bars one and three. Using 1/16th notes we're playing a quick two-note phrase that spans the bar line and adds a little urgency to the feel.

Notice, however, that most of bar two is left empty. The temptation to fill space is a strong one, for sure, but leaving this space will allow us room to add fills later. This is one of the most important ways in which we can make a short loop sound like a much longer one.

This part of the tune has a tonal centre of B Minor. Bar four of each block adds the classic turnaround of the iv chord, suggesting an Em7.

Example 8a

This example shows a variation to the main theme riff, leading into a change of feel as we move from fingerstyle technique to slapping.

Bar one has the riff played fingerstyle and in bar two we introduce the first fill. This acts as a springboard into the second half of the main theme.

For a darker sound, the fill uses notes from the B Dorian scale, rather than the B Minor scale. It starts with a half-step hammer-on to the b7 (A) of the underlying Bm7 harmony and ends on the 3rd (D) and includes the octave D to give it a little spike.

To mark a lift in the second half of the main theme, I then change to slapping the riff. The second time around the slapped version, I add some popped notes for variation.

Example 8b

We're about to move into a different section of the tune and here the arrangement leaves space for a solo bass fill. In the next part of the tune, the harmony will be based around an A7 vamp, so it made sense to mark this with a lick that stepped down from one tonal centre to the next.

This idea of playing a phrase with a repeating rhythm that is then moved around the fretboard is an influence drawn from many of my favourite jazz-funk recordings.

Example 8c

The new section of the tune needs a new idea. We're working over an A7 vamp, and the new motif here uses chromatic approaches to target chord tones.

I bounce the line around the root (A) and b7 (G) of the chord, using a combination of chromatics and open strings. As usual, I try to add some moments of interest with little stabs of "ear candy". One such example is the popped B to C# phrase at the end of bar three. Played in the upper register, this is a 9th to 10th interval movement.

The fill in bar four that finishes each four-bar block is a stylistically favourite sound of mine. Much the same as blues players will blur and jump between major and minor tonalities, here instead of using the A Mixolydian scale to play a line over A7, we're using A Dorian.

The lick implies the 9th (B), 3rd (C) and b7 (G) of an Am7 chord, followed by the 6th (F#) then back to the 3rd. The latter F# to C movement creates a nice tritone tension.

If we think in terms of the A7 harmony underneath this lick, the idea of superimposing Am7 chord tones over A7 creates some interesting intervals. In terms of A7, B is the 9th, C becomes the #9, and G is the b7, while F# is the 13th.

Example 8d

In the next example, the final theme idea is introduced. In this outro section we are vamping between Am and F chords. To make this simple transition I move from A to G to F, but occasionally embellish that movement with a passing Gb, as in bar one.

Or, I might suggest a ii – V movement by playing G then C (i.e., implying Gm – C7 – F). The fills here are based around the A Minor Pentatonic scale.

This line establishes the groove as being a two-bar repetition, with the A root note played on beat 1, and the chord change to F being played with an 1/8th note push at the end of the same bar.

Look out for the ghost note rake in bar eight. This is arranged as if I were playing the octave, 5th and root of an F chord, and is followed by a classic A Minor Pentatonic funk phrase.

Example 8e

Example 8f is a busier variation on the final theme. We retain the core idea, but the rhythmic intensity is ramped up with 1/16th note variations and muted notes.

Example 8f

Below is the study piece in full. Before we get started, let me highlight just a couple more ideas that were played during the outro of this tune.

In bar 96 I play a fill that establishes a kind of theme that I later expand on. The idea is a simple one: to embellish the movement from F to Am using a passing G note (or implied chord). The lick is two four-note phrases played with 1/16th notes. First, you'll play a root-5th-octave pattern in F, then hammer onto a G note on the D string. Then you'll need to quickly jump back to the G on the E string, 3rd fret and repeat the same pattern.

The execution of the lick is a little tricky at full tempo and I find it easiest to play the low F note on the first fret with my first finger, then jump up to the 3rd fret and play the notes on adjacent strings both with the first finger, hammering onto the 5th fret with the second finger. If you decide to finger it this way, you'll roll your first finger from the A to D strings at the 3rd fret. However, feel free to experiment with other fingerings if this doesn't feel good to you.

Notice that at the beginning of bar 97 I leave a rest on beat 1, before playing a descending octave-5th-root figure. I like to introduce a "breath" in the music after a burst of something busy to break up the phrasing.

Now look ahead to bar 104 and you'll see that line is an expansion of the idea in bar 96. Instead of starting on beat 3 here, I play a similar phrase from the 1/8th note push, so that it covers beat 1. Then the root-5th-ocatve motif climbs through F, G, A and Bb, before finishing with a slide from the octave Bb down a half step to the A. You can probably that see my approach is simply embellishing an ascent of the first four notes of the F Major scale. You'll hear a similar take on this idea in bar 120.

I try to add more interest to the bassline in bars 105-106. First of all, we leave some space before a wide slide from high up (descending from the C note on the 17th fret). Then in bar 106 we have a change of dynamic with some harmonics.

The first harmonic "chord" uses the natural harmonics at the 7th fret and combines them with an F bass note to sound an F6 chord (its 3rd and 6th are the harmonic notes). Then, I imply a C9 passing chord to lead into the Am in bar 107. The C9 is hinted at using just G and D natural harmonics at the 5th fret.

Bars 109-110 feature some simple but effective 1/16th note phrases using A Minor then F Major Pentatonic. Bar 116 features more F Major Pentatonic phases, and you'll often hear two staccato 1/16th notes followed by a 1/16th note hammer-on. That always feel very comfortable on bass and I like the sound.

There is a similar pentatonic fill over the F Major chord in bar 24. Here I'm superimposing the A Minor Pentatonic scale over an F chord. A Minor Pentatonic and F Major Pentatonic have four notes in common, and playing the minor pentatonic scale introduces an E note, which implies the sound of Fmaj7. Notice again the use of two plucked 1/16th notes before a hammer-on.

As the track plays through the final bars, I also add occasional pops and the odd slap, all to keep excitement and sparkle, but balanced with a few moments of space.

I hope you enjoy working through it!

Example 8g – "My Pleasure"

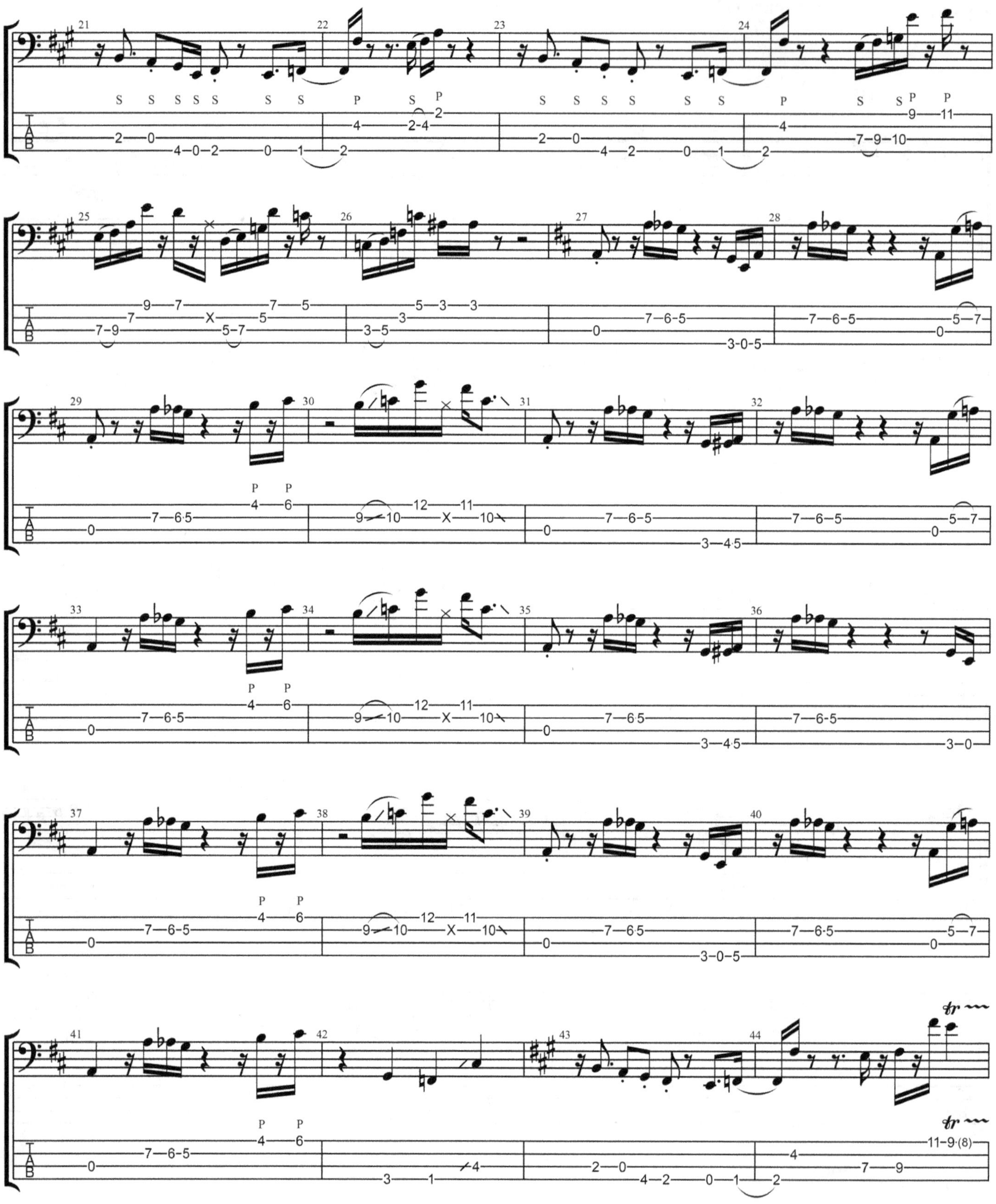

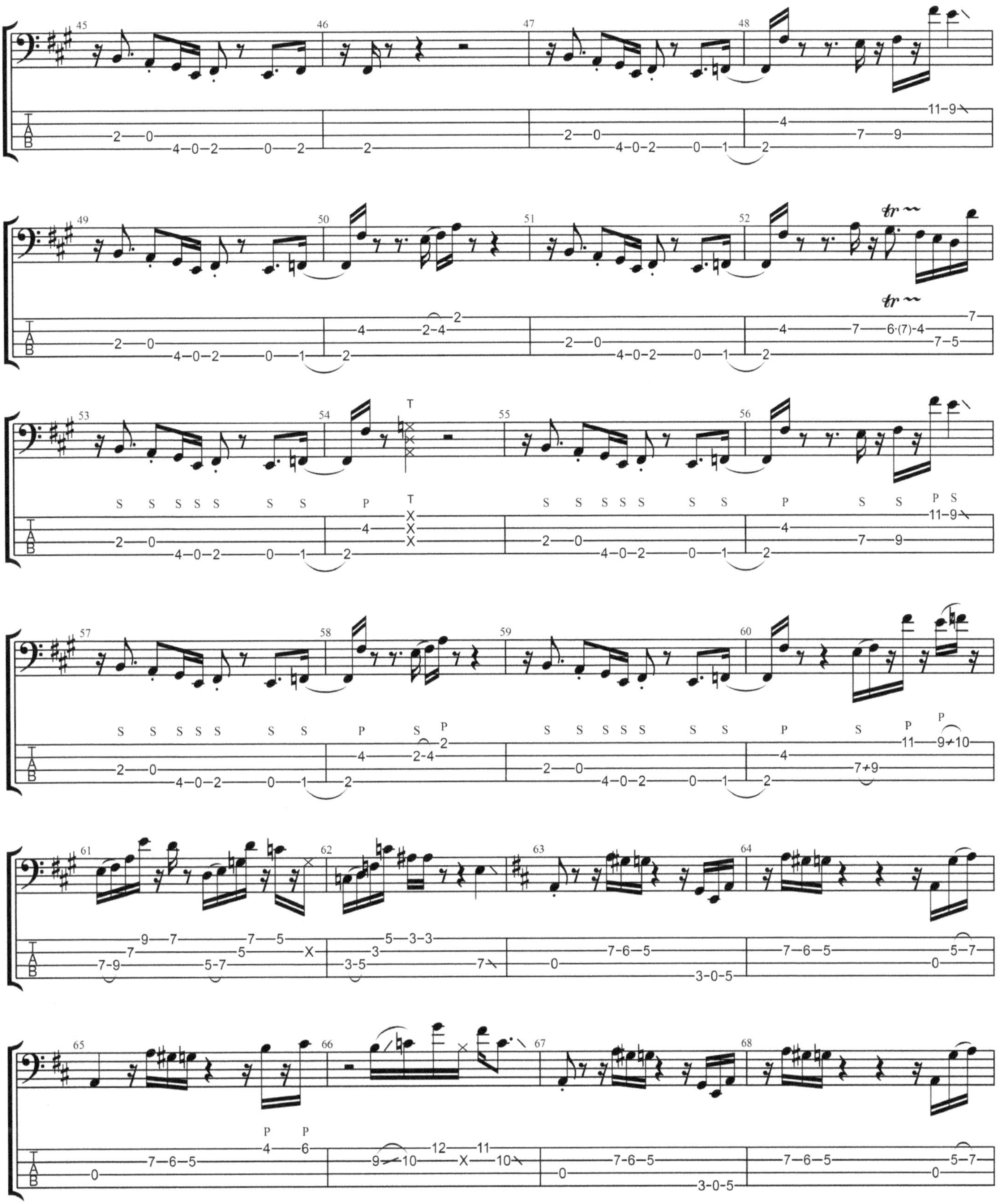

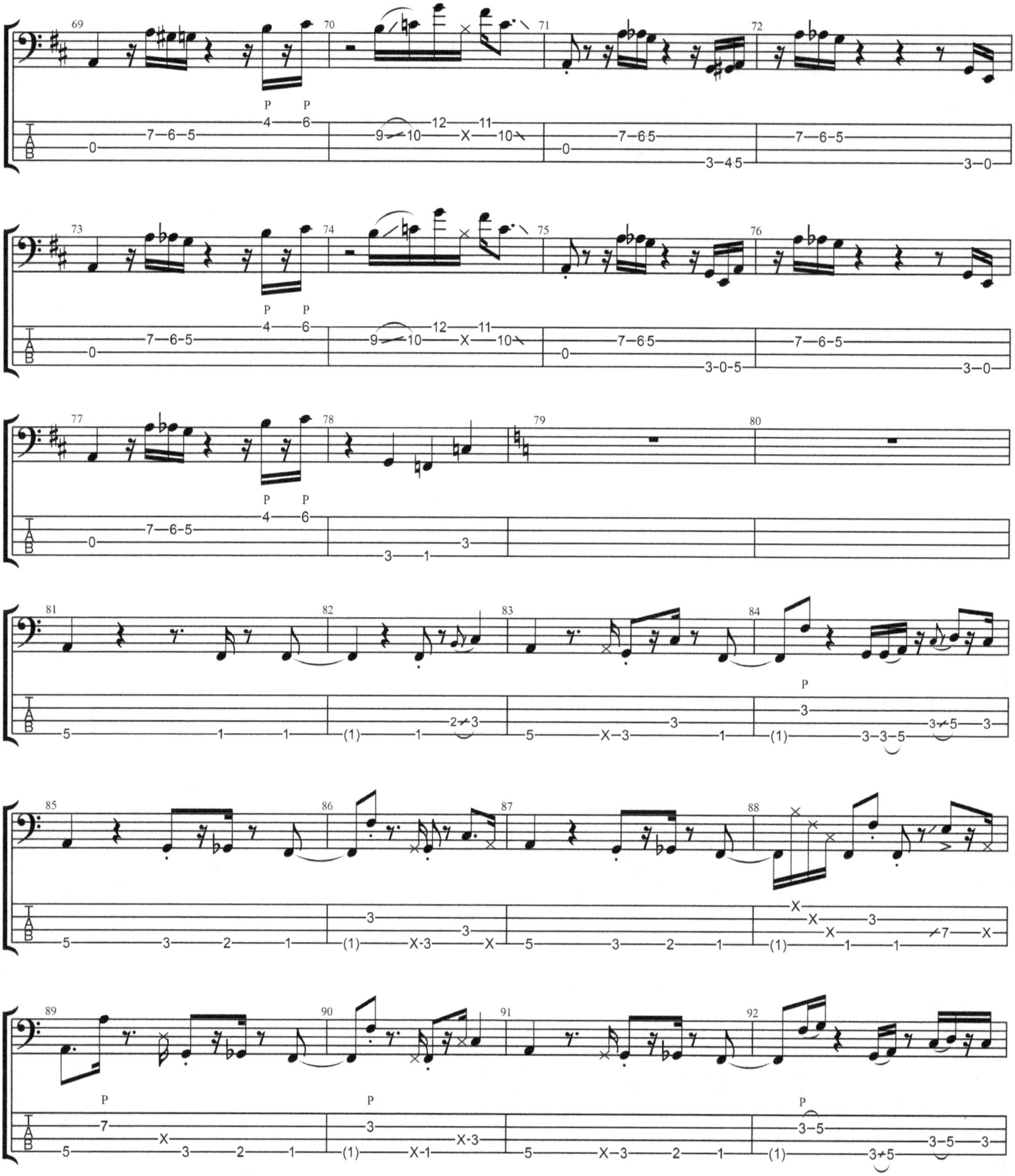

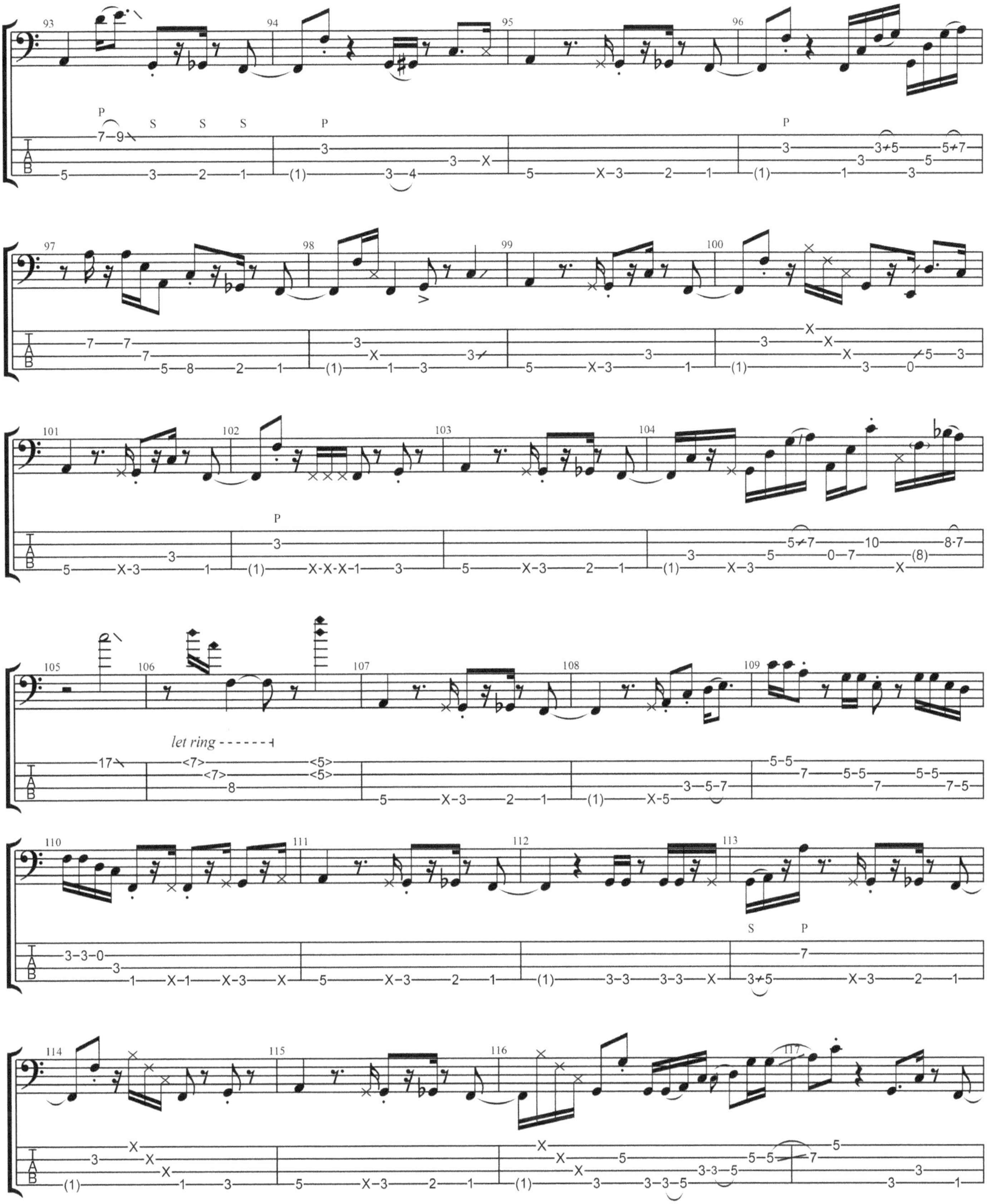
let ring

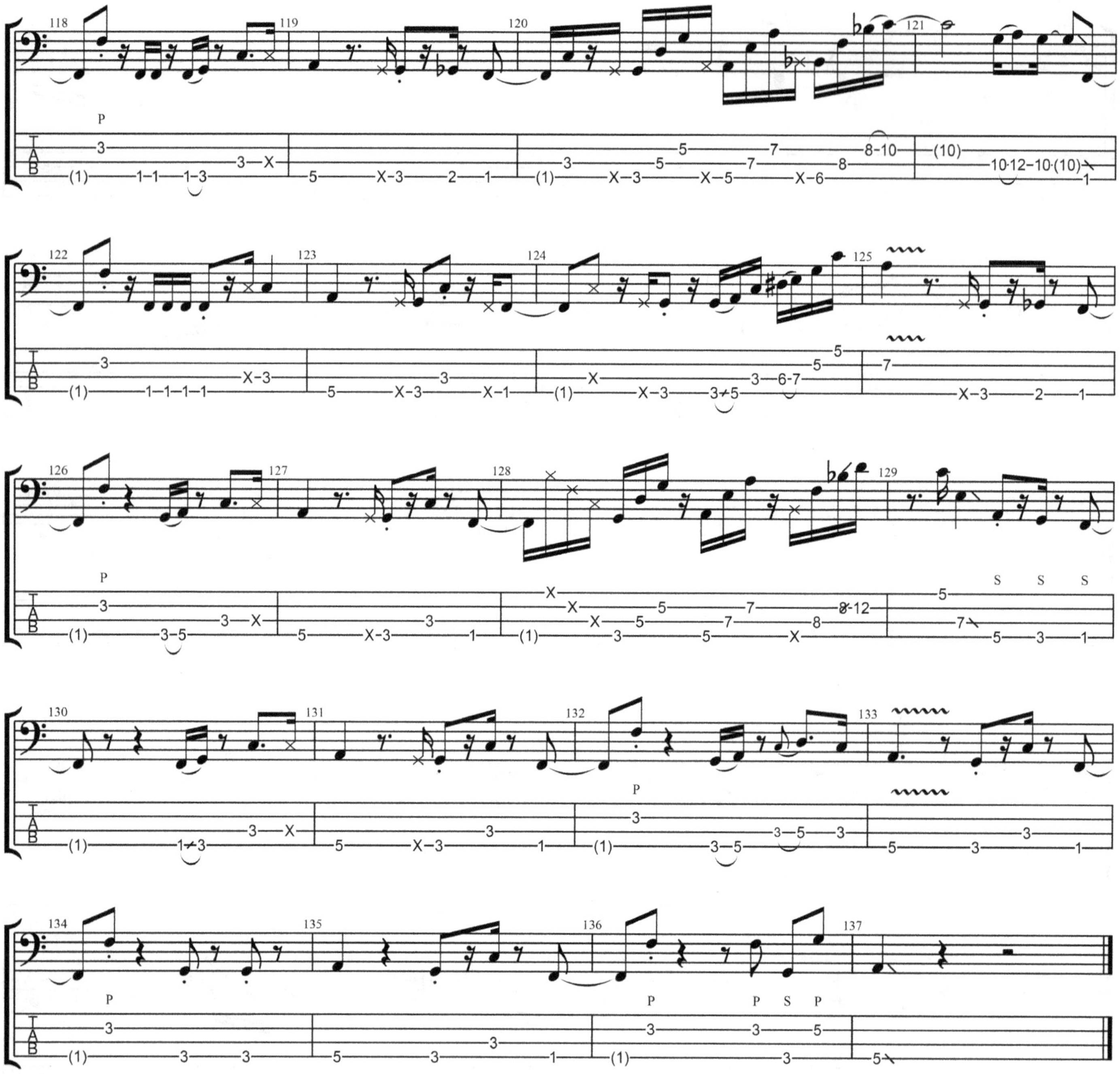

Conclusion

The study tune you've just worked through, and all the lines contained in this book, include "suggestions" and examples of how I approach improvising and composing bass parts. Some are the kind of ideas I use as warm-up drills, while others are examples of solutions I've found to help me become smoother and more consistent with my feel and groove. Others outline the targets I have in mind when writing catchy, creative parts.

With that in mind, the most important advice I can leave you with is to try and absorb the "intent" with which the ideas were written, so that you can apply the ideas and create your own variations to add to your playing vocabulary.

To keep improving, record yourself playing, whether that's just a basic phone recording or using a DAW such as GarageBand or Logic, etc. Listening to yourself on a recording will tell you so much more about your playing than what you *think* you are playing!

Vary your practice to include working with a metronome or drum machine, but importantly, also play *without* any tempo assistance. Aim to develop an independent feel and groove that makes you want to move, dance, or engage the classic "chicken" bass neck! Always embrace the groove and don't be afraid to lock it down.

I'd like to thank and acknowledge all the great bassists and other musicians/artists who have influenced me and continue to inspire. And, finally, to you: I really hope you've found this book helpful and enjoyable. Thank you for your interest and support!

Paul.

Conclusion

Paul has been a professional musician for over 35 years.

In 2005, he joined UK band Jamiroquai and has featured on all the band's recordings and live performances since.

As well as Jamiroquai, he is also known for playing in the Annie Lennox band over a number of years. Other recording and/or live credits include Tina Turner, Bryan Ferry, Tom Jones, Seal and George Michael.

As a recording musician and live performer, Paul has played with a number of U.S. icons such as Sister Sledge and Lamont Dozier, as well as UK R&B legends such as Omar and Mica Paris. He has also played with Jazz-Funk acts like Brother Strut, Down to the Bone and Jeff Lorber, plus a long list of high profile UK and international chart topping acts.

This work has taken him around the world over many years and he has performed at venues ranging from Madison Square Gardens and Wembley Arena to The Budokan and Ronnie Scott's, as well as most of the worlds legendary festivals including Glastonbury, Rock in Rio, Montreux Jazz and Coachella.

Paul is also a visiting professor at many UK music colleges and international educational events and has hosted residential Paul Turner Bass Camps in the UK, Spain, Italy and Poland and held Masterclasses throughout the UK as well as in France, Germany, Italy, Ireland, Russia and Finland.

www.paulturnerbass.com

Instagram: **paulturnerbass**

FaceBook: **paulturnerbass**

X: **paulturnerbass**